Apologetics

by

E.G. Cunningham

Finishing Line Press
Georgetown, Kentucky

Apologetics

Copyright © 2017 by E.G. Cunningham
ISBN 978-1-63534-093-8 First Edition
All rights reserved under International and Pan-American Copyright Conventions.
No part of this book may be reproduced in any manner whatsoever without written permission from the publisher, except in the case of brief quotations embodied in critical articles and reviews.

ACKNOWLEDGMENTS

Many thanks to all those who read or spurred these pieces, directly and indirectly. Many thanks to the Bear Hollow Zoo and to The State Botanical Garden of Georgia. Thank you to Jim Galvin, Tony Hoagland, Peter Gizzi, Cole Swensen, and the Iowa Writers' Workshop. Thank you to Judith Cofer, Ed Pavlić, and Andrew Zawacki, and the UGA CWP. To Erina Harris, Lauren Gould, Jane Lewty, Luther Moss, Meagan Wilson, and Mauricio Sierra: thank you for IA and much more. Thank you to Katy and Tracey for the long haul. To Forrest: for berries; to Djuna: for crescent moons. To my family: Christian, Fred, Jessica, Rebecca, and my parents. To Matthew: thank you for it all.

Publisher: Leah Maines

Editor: Christen Kincaid

Cover Art: Iris prismatica Winton, 1884 (YU.031172). Courtesy of the Peabody Museum of Natural History, Division of Botany, Yale University; peabody.yale.edu.

Author Photo: Matthew Nye

Cover Design: E.G. Cunningham

Printed in the USA on acid-free paper.
Order online: www.finishinglinepress.com
        also available on amazon.com

Author inquiries and mail orders:
Finishing Line Press
P. O. Box 1626
Georgetown, Kentucky 40324
U. S. A.

Table of Contents

Aandblom 1

Ayuxwa 15

for Hadley : great & small

[Nature does nothing uselessly.]
—Aristotle

[There is no God, Nature sufficeth unto herself; in no wise hath she need of an author.]
—Marquis de Sade

[I was not prepared: sunset, end of summer. Demonstrations of time as a continuum…]
—Louise Gluck, *Seven Ages*

AANDBLOM

Nature, forgive me.

I

I spend the summer reading. The days
      wash & glare likely tomorrows; my job:
           to track

    the patterns of voices, tragedies, whole
        histories. An impossibility.

& when, at the second
          rush of first light the ignitions
              start up the neighborhood,

I tell myself that I am not
          not contributing by keeping close
             old words in forfeiture of

the spoken world—
    consumer world,
        traffic & business world,
            lunch break when someone else says so world,
                on my feet all day world—

ideals are easiest early in the day

II

We've moved. My significant &
      I. To save money
  & guilt: from a house

      to a cul-de-sac parking lot—
   double-decker apartments, a few stray cats,
      barbed-wire around a swimming pool.

    It's peaceful here, on the outskirts of town
       trapped in by the highway:
  no carrion voices, no radios.

  I imagine the post-human landscape as
        peaceful, &
   not a bit picturesque.

I spend the summer reading:
      kitsch antiquation
        settlements & troubles—
   concentration studies.

      A week passes.

   I meet a neighbor. She says:
       one of the cats is starving—
it's hard for me to tell.

III

One needs a key
                       to move past the chainlink
                                   to lie on vinyl furniture
       in ideas of reference under a Georgian sun

            whispering—do not react too much—

I swim. It's been years : I forget
                 the shock the miracle of
                           keeping my eyes open. I swim
     to confess the covered up the flesh hating years—

unobserved but for an insect drowning in
                                    the deep end

IV

Winter is better. Fall, too :
    death & dying lessened / less redolent
            when weather mirrors the finite hollow

Summer demands. Says :
    now you have everything—
             sun, earth, sky, green comingling with

        the glazed, impressionist plate—now
            that it is easier to survive
              the question becomes
what have you to show for it.

Weeks pass.
        I discover we live near
            a "free" zoo / I read &, at intervals,
    go regularly.

Thursday : two bald eagles
        rip the flesh from tilapia—scales, tendons—
            turkeys enclosed with a doe & a stag
    the woodchuck a forced vegetarian.

            The donation deposit box : empty.

I watch
        for hours—animal orders
            hierarchies prevail : nothing personal
              no reciprocal altruism
& no right action—

        to coo the deer into turning
            to turn my back on the enclosures—
    spectate or abandon / I'm free &
        it's too much, this guilt & fear, to hold together.

V

A search for
        "why do animals eat each other" yields
                        only tautologies—because of

      the food chain; because teeth; because many animals survive on
meat—
        although who would log in
                      simply to answer
"I don't know."

Before I left home
        my family had its own ritual
           with meat—
                every Friday, much against
    the catholic tradition
        we grilled steaks & baked potatoes:

            I trimmed the fat carefully—
          something unseemly, too intimate
                  about an opalescent
slice of another being

VI

On TV,
        the platypus closes its eyelids tight
                underwater, beaking
                          echolation for food—

I spend the summer reading.

Guilt makes it possible
        to forgive, &
                          holds the social group together

In a Super Store, I shuck my own guilt
                onto generic paper products & strangers—
                thinking : I'm not like them
                              thinking : I am

                thinking : did Sam Walton envision
    & passing the rows of dirty aquariums
            the fish suspended in false light
            some of them bloated & dead near the surface—
I think: for children / or: "free" market

to have nothing of substance & to lament the having : a paradox

VII

The radio anchor announces the weather :
                humidity in cascading degrees—no breeze

      The news : an 8 year old boy
              hit by a car
                      while riding his bicycle.
            Parents planning the funeral.

        To deny the natural world
                            the respect it deserves
by acting unnaturally—
            no flesh to my lips no outings with friends—
            the somersault motion of days into evenings
      of nights into days—I spend
                the summer reading the inked blood
of dead men, mostly.

To afford the natural world
                the respect it deserves
                        by regarding its consequences
with a certain detachment
                  requires an I-don't-know-what
                          I'm afraid I might have

VIII

Tulip vines : the hummingbirds
                            dive their solo routines
          onto the porch feeder.

                      For fodder I watch them
              a cutting activity—
as Faulkner once said
                        in the voice of a drowning man:
          the sparrow "flicked off the ledge, and was gone"

I take nature personally
                      which is a kind of betrayal—
     to demand a voice
            where perhaps there isn't one.

IX

The book is called DAWN.
        I imagine any ablution / absolution
                as the injury's opposite.
    In the swimming pool again
        the sky moves lapidary pivots
            my legs dead weight in attempts
                to float

Now the mechanical streaks along
            the highway perimeter
    blur faster / rush the ingress egress which asks
                going somewhere—

I stay put.

X

Memorial Park. Esto perpetua

                the Canadian geese V south

& boomerang toward the treeline.

                                    Oil slicks cut
        gray-on-gray / sky or water—the formation
turning, toward the lake

                one bird downed in the brush—
                      dropped between pines—
a flash & struggle of neck & wing
    & loss of face.

I run toward its supposed presence.
        To distance / to make
                    impersonal : I think sidewalk, pedestrian—
    slow mist of silver & mauve
        the bird visible now in the underbrush

& a lard unloosening
        in my chest, wildly,
                a caw.

XI

Weeks pass. 7 a.m. / June light—the single lane
                                        curves ahead to the right
      I take the five miles alone
                                                don't slow

      On the left the lake burns roan & pearlescent
                      & beyond—the patinas of docked hulls

          spark to fade water : my eye caught
in a net of the lake
         I will to untangle when
                 a pert move in the middle road
                       swerves me back.

It's too late.
             I cut the wheel & the frame esses—
                   the squirrel darts, freezes; I clench :
   my car & the small body make contact

XII

Do I die to give it back—
                        I wish. Motionless, I checked—
    its skull blood limbs stamped eidetic into me
             to try for some other cohesion
                      to recognize some good safe harbor
to bray.

From dirt : negotiate bouquet.
      Short spur of light—then—
                      a week of rain.

XIII

Folded safe.
    && skein doubling
  sun's saffron firing. August closes.

Almost time to admit— what's closed me
    is a doubling-back

an unrequited.

    Reaches out as
        epiphenomena forever & only
   behind my shut face
    a backstroke through spacetime or:

some motion
          to make up for this
    life of the mind.

[The prairie is poisonous but pretty in autumn]
—Hai-Dang Phan, "Apollinaire in Iowa"

AYUXWA

I

My first friend here recommends dior mascara, or

    Ich ich ich ich, Plath says, though meaning something different—

We—M, the Penske, and I—pour like dust
                      onto loess soil / over Devonian age

    to join mourning dove, mink, black paw, lynx,
                              & several towns over

        the German pietists intoned *ecclesiolae in ecclesia*
        perennial mountains &

rejecting sola fide—

Spires. August trees obtuse & citrine,

    we pile boxes into the strange apartment
sleep on the mattress, no sheets—
        wake at noon

                & walk a mile to the tobacco shop.

In the Middle West we expect no red-day slump,
    no Amsterdam : but here we are—

        cued over a pool table
            crooked in a faceless bar, at noon,

    having followed a man
        with filthy nails & guitar strap

        to drink dollar beer / pass a white slip
            along each point of our equilateral.

II

The houses split in mean ice / I gape
    the mute crow the sole turret

        of the place adjacent to the torn out lot

  where teenagers static dirty hands with pop
    & cigarettes / I call the branches 'medicine,'

  I call them 'benign' :
        a few months' decay & we know nothing
of what's to come.

We herd out in February dusk,
    stemware hanging blue in nude *alberi*—

waiting the scab to ready : to shave
    old months from new masks—

    behind my live-it-up face / past the timber frame
the putty river cut into, hardening,

    always on our way to some alcoholic warmth
        to join other supernovas
  in the double-wide bar.

One hundred & seventy-eight years ago—

  men forwarded with flintlocks, with quaint ancestral swords

    near the Des Moines rapids / grey winds

  felled three trees, at least—loosening combs, hives, rank & order

it was called, the nickel plate reads, the Honey War.

III

Those were the corpuscles forming.

That was the knee being fixed.

I think to the snow some years later & far from Iowa,
                               projecting the cut back, having split,
       having

tried to snuff / to quit my breath my quick
                 slowed to the wick of a tamped pulse

cottony & neuronal in the viridian room
the bed my arms legs out of periphery
nothing ticking no clock but the windowed night

                         caving what dreams what dreams my god

the overhead light dusty, on—the scream
not the scream but transcribed someplace deep & vena cava,
the dial tone razoring still air still :
I traced my non-thoughts along one path only—

a slow silver buzz thrummed its way through my head, igniting midnight,
magenta—

the winter mattress tangelo slick
                now the walls paved lambent / I eat the image & its pale
shadow
                                             & go
under—

IV

In an Iowa town on the feathertorn snow on the arch bridge, glued in :
                the firs cloaked & echoing to the insulated dark
      some hundred-year loneliness
              of exposure of silent witness—

      to stand alone in sub-zero black, the glass sky growing
              to feel that this is forever, and ever amen—

the reaped fields sweep their origin song along I-80 & to clefs & fissures beyond :
      perhaps a candle lit a window once,
              or a stack exhaled steam into pitch
          origin song : what is this little orb
      my mother set me on—

Or what diamoned lapels to hang on my Christmas tree trunk :

(American, cauled on a Wednesday, daughter, & aspirant—almost prodigal—son)

      A bend in the knees as I plant my uncopied body squarely on ice
          take my seat in the identity lounge : a unified field
shimmering vitric,
          then onyx ; the corvus corvax imploding

the iowa night motet—the ravens' bodies abstract expressing
          over the clean-sheet ground
                    in lines of French horn shadow—

      dizzy, suddenly. Tired of remote beauty—which is to say
                  all of it, & longing
          for home.

V

The men sit at the bar. They sit cramped in the far left L
    most evenings, they wear impassive
            turmeric-colored faces

One of them,
    a physics professor named N—with a mosquito net beard
    & lennon glasses, he

        tells me how—
           [something I forget]
          gravity & small weights
    I tell him I failed that subject—meanwhile
literati glitter & thrust in high booths,
    we being young aren't thinking of bending, but skin,
blood—

VI

There is the light onto mint paint like every morning,
    there is its glint & ripple across the sheet.

There is the doubled dusk holding its kestrel gaze
    before descending.

That is the sound of
        the buzz the faucet the car horn;
        the clip & scrape of the sole over concrete to work;
        the grocery swarm, an ocean of strangers.

Those are lines, new, indicating toward the mouth, eyes :
    & a new internal error, gambled on.

Those are your hands; you have always had them.

VII

A carcass frozen in subzero woods.

        M and I stumble, almost
                toeing the doe, its hooves its coffee brown
                            its flagstaff tail
                            unmoving. There's no
red here   so why do I see it. Lets go, M says.

The sun splinters over the
        fawn. Our earlier tracks covered in down
                I need someone to make it make sense :

        pitch of the afternoon light, death,
                        cut of the Midwest wind
    I don't care whether it's "natural" or not—
                    where, I ask him.

VIII

When I came here I believed in possibility—what stunned
                             me was a mirrored version of it; right

       where left should be—like any death : the expected thing appearing
           in a form unimagined—

                To hold the landscape rope through Iowa
means future abrasion : I cut
              on ruby glass from the ceramic sent arcing
                        the air, the kitchen
on fire with a blackout self would someday
                      be reminded to me—

never, nevertheless.

IX

Escape from the body when we're begging
                              to keep it. Or would oblivion
    & its step-to be that cogent—
    is it cogency we're wanting / this always-in-control steel plate

    the pert face behind old laissez faire charades—

I couldn't say.
                Several times in Iowa
                       I thought I'd neared it : the not-breath best
                               the pictorial recording
    standing in for my stand in which is to say
                     —it's the timing that's important :

        witness : exhibit A : another spun-out
             love ending in rain on a grassy hill—yes, spring.

    Watch as the furniture enters the storm : bed, dresser, desk
               gleaming in water & polish / stuffed

                     into the trunk & one last turn
before we drive off from the last first home

X

I misunderstood myself. Too much
                      for growing commentary for brick
      or to rub against. Nothing was wrong
                            so I made it—nothing always
                                      the tabled offender—

could pinpoint the slippage the noon my mind waves
                  arrivederci stepping from the tarmac / planed

                            to be a good hearty nationalist
          I don't say the name; I subscribe.

It seems on all of the channels
                  the same hysterical me note—

      the Iowa caucus : us-them is the oldest song
                  in the history of the sung world;

turn it off before my unborn labour sputters out.

XI

Unspent. The Africa problem nowhere Midwest—
                              the stray, the WSJ reports

    break my heart equally—when X won, the poet jumped up :
    champagne, for everyone.

                              They'll claw on, largely unloved
while I burn up these luxuries—
        in a parallel world: a nine-year-old girl in

    Ostia, strapped in her suit on an oily strip
               of beach, not far from Rome.

The apple an approximation—perhaps even
                              a tomato

    to feel dangerous

I culled
        for a year the cyanide kernels; Ayuxwa a word

I didn't know—nor snow, to learn as a kind of insulation:
                              to stiffen up.

E.G. Cunningham was born in Columbia, South Carolina. Her poetry, prose, and reviews have appeared in *The Nation, The Poetry Review, 3:AM Magazine, Drunken Boat, Puerto del Sol, Poetry London,* and other publications. She is a graduate of the Iowa Writers' Workshop and a PhD candidate in Creative Writing at the University of Georgia in Athens. Her full-length poetry collection, *Ex Domestica,* is forthcoming from C&R Press.

www.ingramcontent.com/pod-product-compliance
Lightning Source LLC
LaVergne TN
LVHW041510070426
835507LV00012B/1471